My Word Count

From: _____ to _____

Project: _____

Project: _____

Project: _____

Project: _____

Project: _____

WestWard Books
Payson, Arizona

How This Works

There's nothing fancy or magical with this word count tracker: simply enter the name of the project you are working on (initials are fine), put down the date (and time, if you do writing sprints that day), then begin your writing session by putting in the number of words you already have written on your project. Yes, that's on the SECOND line.

When you finish, put the total word count on the FIRST line. Subtract the second number from the first, and voilá! You have a record of your word count total for that day.

Happy writing!

Project   **Date & Time**

Word Count End: _____

- Word Count Begin: _____

          Total words: _____

                       ॐ ॐ

Project   **Date & Time**

Word Count End: _____

- Word Count Begin: _____

          Total words: _____

                       ॐ ॐ

Project   **Date & Time**

Word Count End: _____

- Word Count Begin: _____

          Total words: _____

                       ॐ ॐ

Project   **Date & Time**

Word Count End: _____

- Word Count Begin: _____

          Total words: _____

                       ॐ ॐ

Project   **Date & Time**

Word Count End: _____

\- Word Count Begin: _____

        Total words: _____

❧❧

Project   **Date & Time**

Word Count End: _____

\- Word Count Begin: _____

        Total words: _____

❧❧

Project   **Date & Time**

Word Count End: _____

\- Word Count Begin: _____

        Total words: _____

❧❧

Project   **Date & Time**

Word Count End: _____

\- Word Count Begin: _____

        Total words: _____

❧❧

Project   **Date & Time**

Word Count End: _____

- Word Count Begin: _____

       Total words: _____

               ❧ ❦

Project   **Date & Time**

Word Count End: _____

- Word Count Begin: _____

       Total words: _____

               ❧ ❦

Project   **Date & Time**

Word Count End: _____

- Word Count Begin: _____

       Total words: _____

               ❧ ❦

Project   **Date & Time**

Word Count End: _____

- Word Count Begin: _____

       Total words: _____

               ❧ ❦

Project   **Date & Time**

Word Count End: _____

- Word Count Begin: _____

         Total words: _____

❧ ❧

Project   **Date & Time**

Word Count End: _____

- Word Count Begin: _____

         Total words: _____

❧ ❧

Project   **Date & Time**

Word Count End: _____

- Word Count Begin: _____

         Total words: _____

❧ ❧

Project   **Date & Time**

Word Count End: _____

- Word Count Begin: _____

         Total words: _____

❧ ❧

Project   **Date & Time**

Word Count End: _____

- Word Count Begin: _____

         Total words: _____

∽ ∾

Project   **Date & Time**

Word Count End: _____

- Word Count Begin: _____

         Total words: _____

∽ ∾

Project   **Date & Time**

Word Count End: _____

- Word Count Begin: _____

         Total words: _____

∽ ∾

Project   **Date & Time**

Word Count End: _____

- Word Count Begin: _____

         Total words: _____

∽ ∾

Project   **Date & Time**

Word Count End: _____

\- Word Count Begin: _____

        Total words: _____

ം◌ ◌ം

Project   **Date & Time**

Word Count End: _____

\- Word Count Begin: _____

        Total words: _____

ം◌ ◌ം

Project   **Date & Time**

Word Count End: _____

\- Word Count Begin: _____

        Total words: _____

ം◌ ◌ം

Project   **Date & Time**

Word Count End: _____

\- Word Count Begin: _____

        Total words: _____

ം◌ ◌ം

Project   **Date & Time**

Word Count End: _____

- Word Count Begin: _____

         Total words: _____

ॐ ॐ

Project   **Date & Time**

Word Count End: _____

- Word Count Begin: _____

         Total words: _____

ॐ ॐ

Project   **Date & Time**

Word Count End: _____

- Word Count Begin: _____

         Total words: _____

ॐ ॐ

Project   **Date & Time**

Word Count End: _____

- Word Count Begin: _____

         Total words: _____

ॐ ॐ

Project   **Date & Time**

Word Count End: _____

- Word Count Begin: _____

       Total words: _____

‿ ◞

Project   **Date & Time**

Word Count End: _____

- Word Count Begin: _____

       Total words: _____

‿ ◞

Project   **Date & Time**

Word Count End: _____

- Word Count Begin: _____

       Total words: _____

‿ ◞

Project   **Date & Time**

Word Count End: _____

- Word Count Begin: _____

       Total words: _____

‿ ◞

Project   **Date & Time**

Word Count End: _____

- Word Count Begin: _____

       Total words: _____

ॐ ॐ

Project   **Date & Time**

Word Count End: _____

- Word Count Begin: _____

       Total words: _____

ॐ ॐ

Project   **Date & Time**

Word Count End: _____

- Word Count Begin: _____

       Total words: _____

ॐ ॐ

Project   **Date & Time**

Word Count End: _____

- Word Count Begin: _____

       Total words: _____

ॐ ॐ

Project   **Date & Time**

Word Count End: _____

- Word Count Begin: _____

      Total words: _____

ॐ ॐ

Project   **Date & Time**

Word Count End: _____

- Word Count Begin: _____

      Total words: _____

ॐ ॐ

Project   **Date & Time**

Word Count End: _____

- Word Count Begin: _____

      Total words: _____

ॐ ॐ

Project   **Date & Time**

Word Count End: _____

- Word Count Begin: _____

      Total words: _____

ॐ ॐ

Project   **Date & Time**

Word Count End: _____

- Word Count Begin: _____

           Total words: _____

ॐ ॐ

Project   **Date & Time**

Word Count End: _____

- Word Count Begin: _____

           Total words: _____

ॐ ॐ

Project   **Date & Time**

Word Count End: _____

- Word Count Begin: _____

           Total words: _____

ॐ ॐ

Project   **Date & Time**

Word Count End: _____

- Word Count Begin: _____

           Total words: _____

ॐ ॐ

Project   **Date & Time**

Word Count End: _____

- Word Count Begin: _____

        Total words: _____

                              ಹ ೕ

Project   **Date & Time**

Word Count End: _____

- Word Count Begin: _____

        Total words: _____

                              ಹ ೕ

Project   **Date & Time**

Word Count End: _____

- Word Count Begin: _____

        Total words: _____

                              ಹ ೕ

Project   **Date & Time**

Word Count End: _____

- Word Count Begin: _____

        Total words: _____

                              ಹ ೕ

Project   **Date & Time**

Word Count End: _____

- Word Count Begin: _____

         Total words: _____

ॐ ॐ

Project   **Date & Time**

Word Count End: _____

- Word Count Begin: _____

         Total words: _____

ॐ ॐ

Project   **Date & Time**

Word Count End: _____

- Word Count Begin: _____

         Total words: _____

ॐ ॐ

Project   **Date & Time**

Word Count End: _____

- Word Count Begin: _____

         Total words: _____

ॐ ॐ

Project   **Date & Time**

Word Count End: _____

- Word Count Begin: _____

   Total words: _____

     ॐ ॐ

Project   **Date & Time**

Word Count End: _____

- Word Count Begin: _____

   Total words: _____

     ॐ ॐ

Project   **Date & Time**

Word Count End: _____

- Word Count Begin: _____

   Total words: _____

     ॐ ॐ

Project   **Date & Time**

Word Count End: _____

- Word Count Begin: _____

   Total words: _____

     ॐ ॐ

Project   **Date & Time**

Word Count End: _____

- Word Count Begin: _____

      Total words: _____

~~~~

Project   **Date & Time**

Word Count End: _____

- Word Count Begin: _____

      Total words: _____

~~~~

Project   **Date & Time**

Word Count End: _____

- Word Count Begin: _____

      Total words: _____

~~~~

Project   **Date & Time**

Word Count End: _____

- Word Count Begin: _____

      Total words: _____

~~~~

Project   **Date & Time**

Word Count End: _____

- Word Count Begin: _____

         Total words: _____

                     ❧ ❧

Project   **Date & Time**

Word Count End: _____

- Word Count Begin: _____

         Total words: _____

                     ❧ ❧

Project   **Date & Time**

Word Count End: _____

- Word Count Begin: _____

         Total words: _____

                     ❧ ❧

Project   **Date & Time**

Word Count End: _____

- Word Count Begin: _____

         Total words: _____

                     ❧ ❧

Project   **Date & Time**

Word Count End: _____

- Word Count Begin: _____

   Total words: _____

❧❧

Project   **Date & Time**

Word Count End: _____

- Word Count Begin: _____

   Total words: _____

❧❧

Project   **Date & Time**

Word Count End: _____

- Word Count Begin: _____

   Total words: _____

❧❧

Project   **Date & Time**

Word Count End: _____

- Word Count Begin: _____

   Total words: _____

❧❧

Project   **Date & Time**

Word Count End: _____

- Word Count Begin: _____

       Total words: _____

છ્ર જ્ઞ

Project   **Date & Time**

Word Count End: _____

- Word Count Begin: _____

       Total words: _____

છ્ર જ્ઞ

Project   **Date & Time**

Word Count End: _____

- Word Count Begin: _____

       Total words: _____

છ્ર જ્ઞ

Project   **Date & Time**

Word Count End: _____

- Word Count Begin: _____

       Total words: _____

છ્ર જ્ઞ

Project   **Date & Time**

Word Count End: _____

- Word Count Begin: _____

       Total words: _____

             ৵ ৶

Project   **Date & Time**

Word Count End: _____

- Word Count Begin: _____

       Total words: _____

             ৵ ৶

Project   **Date & Time**

Word Count End: _____

- Word Count Begin: _____

       Total words: _____

             ৵ ৶

Project   **Date & Time**

Word Count End: _____

- Word Count Begin: _____

       Total words: _____

             ৵ ৶

Project   **Date & Time**

Word Count End: _____

- Word Count Begin: _____

       Total words: _____

ตั้ง ตั้ง

Project   **Date & Time**

Word Count End: _____

- Word Count Begin: _____

       Total words: _____

ตั้ง ตั้ง

Project   **Date & Time**

Word Count End: _____

- Word Count Begin: _____

       Total words: _____

ตั้ง ตั้ง

Project   **Date & Time**

Word Count End: _____

- Word Count Begin: _____

       Total words: _____

ตั้ง ตั้ง

Project   **Date & Time**

Word Count End: _____

- Word Count Begin: _____

           Total words: _____

∞ ∞

Project   **Date & Time**

Word Count End: _____

- Word Count Begin: _____

           Total words: _____

∞ ∞

Project   **Date & Time**

Word Count End: _____

- Word Count Begin: _____

           Total words: _____

∞ ∞

Project   **Date & Time**

Word Count End: _____

- Word Count Begin: _____

           Total words: _____

∞ ∞

Project   **Date & Time**

Word Count End: _____

- Word Count Begin: _____

       Total words: _____

                                 છ ઓ

Project   **Date & Time**

Word Count End: _____

- Word Count Begin: _____

       Total words: _____

                                 છ ઓ

Project   **Date & Time**

Word Count End: _____

- Word Count Begin: _____

       Total words: _____

                                 છ ઓ

Project   **Date & Time**

Word Count End: _____

- Word Count Begin: _____

       Total words: _____

                                 છ ઓ

Project   **Date & Time**

Word Count End: _____

- Word Count Begin: _____

      Total words: _____

ᚷ ᚶ

Project   **Date & Time**

Word Count End: _____

- Word Count Begin: _____

      Total words: _____

ᚷ ᚶ

Project   **Date & Time**

Word Count End: _____

- Word Count Begin: _____

      Total words: _____

ᚷ ᚶ

Project   **Date & Time**

Word Count End: _____

- Word Count Begin: _____

      Total words: _____

ᚷ ᚶ

Project   **Date & Time**

Word Count End: _____

- Word Count Begin: _____

         Total words: _____

                ❧ ❦

Project   **Date & Time**

Word Count End: _____

- Word Count Begin: _____

         Total words: _____

                ❧ ❦

Project   **Date & Time**

Word Count End: _____

- Word Count Begin: _____

         Total words: _____

                ❧ ❦

Project   **Date & Time**

Word Count End: _____

- Word Count Begin: _____

         Total words: _____

                ❧ ❦

Project   **Date & Time**

Word Count End: _____

\- Word Count Begin: _____

         Total words: _____

੭ ੬

Project   **Date & Time**

Word Count End: _____

\- Word Count Begin: _____

         Total words: _____

੭ ੬

Project   **Date & Time**

Word Count End: _____

\- Word Count Begin: _____

         Total words: _____

੭ ੬

Project   **Date & Time**

Word Count End: _____

\- Word Count Begin: _____

         Total words: _____

੭ ੬

Project   **Date & Time**

Word Count End: _____

- Word Count Begin: _____

        Total words: _____

                ∂ ∞

Project   **Date & Time**

Word Count End: _____

- Word Count Begin: _____

        Total words: _____

                ∂ ∞

Project   **Date & Time**

Word Count End: _____

- Word Count Begin: _____

        Total words: _____

                ∂ ∞

Project   **Date & Time**

Word Count End: _____

- Word Count Begin: _____

        Total words: _____

                ∂ ∞

Project   **Date & Time**

Word Count End: _____

- Word Count Begin: _____

           Total words: _____

                ॐ ॐ

Project   **Date & Time**

Word Count End: _____

- Word Count Begin: _____

           Total words: _____

                ॐ ॐ

Project   **Date & Time**

Word Count End: _____

- Word Count Begin: _____

           Total words: _____

                ॐ ॐ

Project   **Date & Time**

Word Count End: _____

- Word Count Begin: _____

           Total words: _____

                ॐ ॐ

Project   **Date & Time**

Word Count End: _____

- Word Count Begin: _____

         Total words: _____

                    ॐ ॐ

Project   **Date & Time**

Word Count End: _____

- Word Count Begin: _____

         Total words: _____

                    ॐ ॐ

Project   **Date & Time**

Word Count End: _____

- Word Count Begin: _____

         Total words: _____

                    ॐ ॐ

Project   **Date & Time**

Word Count End: _____

- Word Count Begin: _____

         Total words: _____

                    ॐ ॐ

Project   **Date & Time**

Word Count End: _____

- Word Count Begin: _____

         Total words: _____

                          ॐ ॐ

Project   **Date & Time**

Word Count End: _____

- Word Count Begin: _____

         Total words: _____

                          ॐ ॐ

Project   **Date & Time**

Word Count End: _____

- Word Count Begin: _____

         Total words: _____

                          ॐ ॐ

Project   **Date & Time**

Word Count End: _____

- Word Count Begin: _____

         Total words: _____

                          ॐ ॐ

Project   **Date & Time**

Word Count End: _____

- Word Count Begin: _____

            Total words: _____

                        ⊱ ⊰

Project   **Date & Time**

Word Count End: _____

- Word Count Begin: _____

            Total words: _____

                        ⊱ ⊰

Project   **Date & Time**

Word Count End: _____

- Word Count Begin: _____

            Total words: _____

                        ⊱ ⊰

Project   **Date & Time**

Word Count End: _____

- Word Count Begin: _____

            Total words: _____

                        ⊱ ⊰

Project   **Date & Time**

Word Count End: _____

- Word Count Begin: _____

                    Total words: _____

ॐ ॐ

Project   **Date & Time**

Word Count End: _____

- Word Count Begin: _____

                    Total words: _____

ॐ ॐ

Project   **Date & Time**

Word Count End: _____

- Word Count Begin: _____

                    Total words: _____

ॐ ॐ

Project   **Date & Time**

Word Count End: _____

- Word Count Begin: _____

                    Total words: _____

ॐ ॐ

Project   **Date & Time**

Word Count End: _____

- Word Count Begin: _____

      Total words: _____

જી ન્લ

Project   **Date & Time**

Word Count End: _____

- Word Count Begin: _____

      Total words: _____

જી ન્લ

Project   **Date & Time**

Word Count End: _____

- Word Count Begin: _____

      Total words: _____

જી ન્લ

Project   **Date & Time**

Word Count End: _____

- Word Count Begin: _____

      Total words: _____

જી ન્લ

Project   **Date & Time**

Word Count End: _____

- Word Count Begin: _____

         Total words: _____

                            ✌ ✌

Project   **Date & Time**

Word Count End: _____

- Word Count Begin: _____

         Total words: _____

                            ✌ ✌

Project   **Date & Time**

Word Count End: _____

- Word Count Begin: _____

         Total words: _____

                            ✌ ✌

Project   **Date & Time**

Word Count End: _____

- Word Count Begin: _____

         Total words: _____

                            ✌ ✌

Project   **Date & Time**

Word Count End: _____

- Word Count Begin: _____

       Total words: _____

          ✿ ❧

Project   **Date & Time**

Word Count End: _____

- Word Count Begin: _____

       Total words: _____

          ✿ ❧

Project   **Date & Time**

Word Count End: _____

- Word Count Begin: _____

       Total words: _____

          ✿ ❧

Project   **Date & Time**

Word Count End: _____

- Word Count Begin: _____

       Total words: _____

          ✿ ❧

Project   **Date & Time**

Word Count End: _____

- Word Count Begin: _____

        Total words: _____

ॐ ॐ

Project   **Date & Time**

Word Count End: _____

- Word Count Begin: _____

        Total words: _____

ॐ ॐ

Project   **Date & Time**

Word Count End: _____

- Word Count Begin: _____

        Total words: _____

ॐ ॐ

Project   **Date & Time**

Word Count End: _____

- Word Count Begin: _____

        Total words: _____

ॐ ॐ

Project   **Date & Time**

Word Count End: _____

- Word Count Begin: _____

        Total words: _____

ॐ ॐ

Project   **Date & Time**

Word Count End: _____

- Word Count Begin: _____

        Total words: _____

ॐ ॐ

Project   **Date & Time**

Word Count End: _____

- Word Count Begin: _____

        Total words: _____

ॐ ॐ

Project   **Date & Time**

Word Count End: _____

- Word Count Begin: _____

        Total words: _____

ॐ ॐ

Project   **Date & Time**

Word Count End: _____

- Word Count Begin: _____

             Total words: _____

👌 👌

Project   **Date & Time**

Word Count End: _____

- Word Count Begin: _____

             Total words: _____

👌 👌

Project   **Date & Time**

Word Count End: _____

- Word Count Begin: _____

             Total words: _____

👌 👌

Project   **Date & Time**

Word Count End: _____

- Word Count Begin: _____

             Total words: _____

👌 👌

Project   **Date & Time**

Word Count End: _____

- Word Count Begin: _____

      Total words: _____

 প্র ৵

Project   **Date & Time**

Word Count End: _____

- Word Count Begin: _____

      Total words: _____

 প্র ৵

Project   **Date & Time**

Word Count End: _____

- Word Count Begin: _____

      Total words: _____

 প্র ৵

Project   **Date & Time**

Word Count End: _____

- Word Count Begin: _____

      Total words: _____

 প্র ৵

Project   **Date & Time**

Word Count End: _____

- Word Count Begin: _____

        Total words: _____

ॐ ৪৯

Project   **Date & Time**

Word Count End: _____

- Word Count Begin: _____

        Total words: _____

ॐ ৪৯

Project   **Date & Time**

Word Count End: _____

- Word Count Begin: _____

        Total words: _____

ॐ ৪৯

Project   **Date & Time**

Word Count End: _____

- Word Count Begin: _____

        Total words: _____

ॐ ৪৯

Project   **Date & Time**

Word Count End: _____

\- Word Count Begin: _____

            Total words: _____

ॐ ॐ

Project   **Date & Time**

Word Count End: _____

\- Word Count Begin: _____

            Total words: _____

ॐ ॐ

Project   **Date & Time**

Word Count End: _____

\- Word Count Begin: _____

            Total words: _____

ॐ ॐ

Project   **Date & Time**

Word Count End: _____

\- Word Count Begin: _____

            Total words: _____

ॐ ॐ

Project   **Date & Time**

Word Count End: _____

- Word Count Begin: _____

       Total words: _____

∽ ∾

Project   **Date & Time**

Word Count End: _____

- Word Count Begin: _____

       Total words: _____

∽ ∾

Project   **Date & Time**

Word Count End: _____

- Word Count Begin: _____

       Total words: _____

∽ ∾

Project   **Date & Time**

Word Count End: _____

- Word Count Begin: _____

       Total words: _____

∽ ∾

Project   **Date & Time**

Word Count End: _____

- Word Count Begin: _____

        Total words: _____

ॐ ॐ

Project   **Date & Time**

Word Count End: _____

- Word Count Begin: _____

        Total words: _____

ॐ ॐ

Project   **Date & Time**

Word Count End: _____

- Word Count Begin: _____

        Total words: _____

ॐ ॐ

Project   **Date & Time**

Word Count End: _____

- Word Count Begin: _____

        Total words: _____

ॐ ॐ

Project   **Date & Time**

Word Count End: _____

- Word Count Begin: _____

    Total words: _____

࿊ ࿊

Project   **Date & Time**

Word Count End: _____

- Word Count Begin: _____

    Total words: _____

࿊ ࿊

Project   **Date & Time**

Word Count End: _____

- Word Count Begin: _____

    Total words: _____

࿊ ࿊

Project   **Date & Time**

Word Count End: _____

- Word Count Begin: _____

    Total words: _____

࿊ ࿊

Project   **Date & Time**

Word Count End: _____

- Word Count Begin: _____

       Total words: _____

ॐ ॐ

Project   **Date & Time**

Word Count End: _____

- Word Count Begin: _____

       Total words: _____

ॐ ॐ

Project   **Date & Time**

Word Count End: _____

- Word Count Begin: _____

       Total words: _____

ॐ ॐ

Project   **Date & Time**

Word Count End: _____

- Word Count Begin: _____

       Total words: _____

ॐ ॐ

Project   **Date & Time**

Word Count End: _____

- Word Count Begin: _____

       Total words: _____

                     ࿎ ࿎

Project   **Date & Time**

Word Count End: _____

- Word Count Begin: _____

       Total words: _____

                     ࿎ ࿎

Project   **Date & Time**

Word Count End: _____

- Word Count Begin: _____

       Total words: _____

                     ࿎ ࿎

Project   **Date & Time**

Word Count End: _____

- Word Count Begin: _____

       Total words: _____

                     ࿎ ࿎

Project　　　　　　　　**Date & Time**

Word Count End: _____

- Word Count Begin: _____

　　　　Total words: _____

ॐ ॐ

Project　　　　　　　　**Date & Time**

Word Count End: _____

- Word Count Begin: _____

　　　　Total words: _____

ॐ ॐ

Project　　　　　　　　**Date & Time**

Word Count End: _____

- Word Count Begin: _____

　　　　Total words: _____

ॐ ॐ

Project　　　　　　　　**Date & Time**

Word Count End: _____

- Word Count Begin: _____

　　　　Total words: _____

ॐ ॐ

Project   **Date & Time**

Word Count End: _____

\- Word Count Begin: _____

          Total words: _____

                 ৯ৎ ৶

Project   **Date & Time**

Word Count End: _____

\- Word Count Begin: _____

          Total words: _____

                 ৯ৎ ৶

Project   **Date & Time**

Word Count End: _____

\- Word Count Begin: _____

          Total words: _____

                 ৯ৎ ৶

Project   **Date & Time**

Word Count End: _____

\- Word Count Begin: _____

          Total words: _____

                 ৯ৎ ৶

Project   **Date & Time**

Word Count End: _____

- Word Count Begin: _____

       Total words: _____

ॐ ॐ

Project   **Date & Time**

Word Count End: _____

- Word Count Begin: _____

       Total words: _____

ॐ ॐ

Project   **Date & Time**

Word Count End: _____

- Word Count Begin: _____

       Total words: _____

ॐ ॐ

Project   **Date & Time**

Word Count End: _____

- Word Count Begin: _____

       Total words: _____

ॐ ॐ

Project   **Date & Time**

Word Count End: _____

- Word Count Begin: _____

       Total words: _____

ॐ ॐ

Project   **Date & Time**

Word Count End: _____

- Word Count Begin: _____

       Total words: _____

ॐ ॐ

Project   **Date & Time**

Word Count End: _____

- Word Count Begin: _____

       Total words: _____

ॐ ॐ

Project   **Date & Time**

Word Count End: _____

- Word Count Begin: _____

       Total words: _____

ॐ ॐ

Project   **Date & Time**

Word Count End: _____

- Word Count Begin: _____

       Total words: _____

        ১৯ ৩৯

Project   **Date & Time**

Word Count End: _____

- Word Count Begin: _____

       Total words: _____

        ১৯ ৩৯

Project   **Date & Time**

Word Count End: _____

- Word Count Begin: _____

       Total words: _____

        ১৯ ৩৯

Project   **Date & Time**

Word Count End: _____

- Word Count Begin: _____

       Total words: _____

        ১৯ ৩৯

Project   **Date & Time**

Word Count End: _____

- Word Count Begin: _____

        Total words: _____

                         ❧ ❦

Project   **Date & Time**

Word Count End: _____

- Word Count Begin: _____

        Total words: _____

                         ❧ ❦

Project   **Date & Time**

Word Count End: _____

- Word Count Begin: _____

        Total words: _____

                         ❧ ❦

Project   **Date & Time**

Word Count End: _____

- Word Count Begin: _____

        Total words: _____

                         ❧ ❦

Project   **Date & Time**

Word Count End: _____

- Word Count Begin: _____

        Total words: _____

ॐ ◈

Project   **Date & Time**

Word Count End: _____

- Word Count Begin: _____

        Total words: _____

ॐ ◈

Project   **Date & Time**

Word Count End: _____

- Word Count Begin: _____

        Total words: _____

ॐ ◈

Project   **Date & Time**

Word Count End: _____

- Word Count Begin: _____

        Total words: _____

ॐ ◈

Project   **Date & Time**

Word Count End: _____

- Word Count Begin: _____

        Total words: _____

            ❧ ☙

Project   **Date & Time**

Word Count End: _____

- Word Count Begin: _____

        Total words: _____

            ❧ ☙

Project   **Date & Time**

Word Count End: _____

- Word Count Begin: _____

        Total words: _____

            ❧ ☙

Project   **Date & Time**

Word Count End: _____

- Word Count Begin: _____

        Total words: _____

            ❧ ☙

Project   **Date & Time**

Word Count End: _____

- Word Count Begin: _____

       Total words: _____

ॐ ॐ

Project   **Date & Time**

Word Count End: _____

- Word Count Begin: _____

       Total words: _____

ॐ ॐ

Project   **Date & Time**

Word Count End: _____

- Word Count Begin: _____

       Total words: _____

ॐ ॐ

Project   **Date & Time**

Word Count End: _____

- Word Count Begin: _____

       Total words: _____

ॐ ॐ

Project   **Date & Time**

Word Count End: _____

- Word Count Begin: _____

      Total words: _____

⇛ ⇚

Project   **Date & Time**

Word Count End: _____

- Word Count Begin: _____

      Total words: _____

⇛ ⇚

Project   **Date & Time**

Word Count End: _____

- Word Count Begin: _____

      Total words: _____

⇛ ⇚

Project   **Date & Time**

Word Count End: _____

- Word Count Begin: _____

      Total words: _____

⇛ ⇚

Project   **Date & Time**

Word Count End: _____

- Word Count Begin: _____

       Total words: _____

ào ·ó

Project   **Date & Time**

Word Count End: _____

- Word Count Begin: _____

       Total words: _____

ào ·ó

Project   **Date & Time**

Word Count End: _____

- Word Count Begin: _____

       Total words: _____

ào ·ó

Project   **Date & Time**

Word Count End: _____

- Word Count Begin: _____

       Total words: _____

ào ·ó

Project   **Date & Time**

Word Count End: _____

- Word Count Begin: _____

    Total words: _____

∶ ∷

Project   **Date & Time**

Word Count End: _____

- Word Count Begin: _____

    Total words: _____

∶ ∷

Project   **Date & Time**

Word Count End: _____

- Word Count Begin: _____

    Total words: _____

∶ ∷

Project   **Date & Time**

Word Count End: _____

- Word Count Begin: _____

    Total words: _____

∶ ∷

Project   **Date & Time**

Word Count End: _____

- Word Count Begin: _____

        Total words: _____

                  ৎ৶ ৶৹

Project   **Date & Time**

Word Count End: _____

- Word Count Begin: _____

        Total words: _____

                  ৎ৶ ৶৹

Project   **Date & Time**

Word Count End: _____

- Word Count Begin: _____

        Total words: _____

                  ৎ৶ ৶৹

Project   **Date & Time**

Word Count End: _____

- Word Count Begin: _____

        Total words: _____

                  ৎ৶ ৶৹

Project   **Date & Time**

Word Count End: _____

- Word Count Begin: _____

   Total words: _____

જ ✖

Project   **Date & Time**

Word Count End: _____

- Word Count Begin: _____

   Total words: _____

જ ✖

Project   **Date & Time**

Word Count End: _____

- Word Count Begin: _____

   Total words: _____

જ ✖

Project   **Date & Time**

Word Count End: _____

- Word Count Begin: _____

   Total words: _____

જ ✖

Project   **Date & Time**

Word Count End: _____

- Word Count Begin: _____

     Total words: _____

ॐ ॐ

Project   **Date & Time**

Word Count End: _____

- Word Count Begin: _____

     Total words: _____

ॐ ॐ

Project   **Date & Time**

Word Count End: _____

- Word Count Begin: _____

     Total words: _____

ॐ ॐ

Project   **Date & Time**

Word Count End: _____

- Word Count Begin: _____

     Total words: _____

ॐ ॐ

Project   **Date & Time**

Word Count End: _____

- Word Count Begin: _____

       Total words: _____

             ෨ ෩

Project   **Date & Time**

Word Count End: _____

- Word Count Begin: _____

       Total words: _____

             ෨ ෩

Project   **Date & Time**

Word Count End: _____

- Word Count Begin: _____

       Total words: _____

             ෨ ෩

Project   **Date & Time**

Word Count End: _____

- Word Count Begin: _____

       Total words: _____

             ෨ ෩

Project   **Date & Time**

Word Count End: _____

- Word Count Begin: _____

        Total words: _____

ﾞﾞﾞﾞﾞﾞﾞﾞﾞﾞ

Project   **Date & Time**

Word Count End: _____

- Word Count Begin: _____

        Total words: _____

ﾞﾞﾞﾞﾞﾞﾞﾞﾞﾞ

Project   **Date & Time**

Word Count End: _____

- Word Count Begin: _____

        Total words: _____

ﾞﾞﾞﾞﾞﾞﾞﾞﾞﾞ

Project   **Date & Time**

Word Count End: _____

- Word Count Begin: _____

        Total words: _____

ﾞﾞﾞﾞﾞﾞﾞﾞﾞﾞ

Project   **Date & Time**

Word Count End: _____

- Word Count Begin: _____

          Total words: _____

                    ❧ ❦

Project   **Date & Time**

Word Count End: _____

- Word Count Begin: _____

          Total words: _____

                    ❧ ❦

Project   **Date & Time**

Word Count End: _____

- Word Count Begin: _____

          Total words: _____

                    ❧ ❦

Project   **Date & Time**

Word Count End: _____

- Word Count Begin: _____

          Total words: _____

                    ❧ ❦

Project   **Date & Time**

Word Count End: _____

- Word Count Begin: _____

        Total words: _____

                 ৵ ৶

Project   **Date & Time**

Word Count End: _____

- Word Count Begin: _____

        Total words: _____

                 ৵ ৶

Project   **Date & Time**

Word Count End: _____

- Word Count Begin: _____

        Total words: _____

                 ৵ ৶

Project   **Date & Time**

Word Count End: _____

- Word Count Begin: _____

        Total words: _____

                 ৵ ৶

Project   **Date & Time**

Word Count End: _____

- Word Count Begin: _____

        Total words: _____

ംഃ ഃം

Project   **Date & Time**

Word Count End: _____

- Word Count Begin: _____

        Total words: _____

ംഃ ഃം

Project   **Date & Time**

Word Count End: _____

- Word Count Begin: _____

        Total words: _____

ംഃ ഃം

Project   **Date & Time**

Word Count End: _____

- Word Count Begin: _____

        Total words: _____

ംഃ ഃം

Project   **Date & Time**

Word Count End: _____

- Word Count Begin: _____

Total words: _____

ॐ ॐ

Project   **Date & Time**

Word Count End: _____

- Word Count Begin: _____

Total words: _____

ॐ ॐ

Project   **Date & Time**

Word Count End: _____

- Word Count Begin: _____

Total words: _____

ॐ ॐ

Project   **Date & Time**

Word Count End: _____

- Word Count Begin: _____

Total words: _____

ॐ ॐ

Project   **Date & Time**

Word Count End: _____

- Word Count Begin: _____

        Total words: _____

❧ ❦

Project   **Date & Time**

Word Count End: _____

- Word Count Begin: _____

        Total words: _____

❧ ❦

Project   **Date & Time**

Word Count End: _____

- Word Count Begin: _____

        Total words: _____

❧ ❦

Project   **Date & Time**

Word Count End: _____

- Word Count Begin: _____

        Total words: _____

❧ ❦

Project   **Date & Time**

Word Count End: _____

- Word Count Begin: _____

     Total words: _____

                      ॐ ॐ

Project   **Date & Time**

Word Count End: _____

- Word Count Begin: _____

     Total words: _____

                      ॐ ॐ

Project   **Date & Time**

Word Count End: _____

- Word Count Begin: _____

     Total words: _____

                      ॐ ॐ

Project   **Date & Time**

Word Count End: _____

- Word Count Begin: _____

     Total words: _____

                      ॐ ॐ

Project   **Date & Time**

Word Count End: _____

- Word Count Begin: _____

       Total words: _____

                 ক্ত ক্ত

Project   **Date & Time**

Word Count End: _____

- Word Count Begin: _____

       Total words: _____

                 ক্ত ক্ত

Project   **Date & Time**

Word Count End: _____

- Word Count Begin: _____

       Total words: _____

                 ক্ত ক্ত

Project   **Date & Time**

Word Count End: _____

- Word Count Begin: _____

       Total words: _____

                 ক্ত ক্ত

Project   **Date & Time**

Word Count End: _____

- Word Count Begin: _____

          Total words: _____

                        ಹ ೖ

Project   **Date & Time**

Word Count End: _____

- Word Count Begin: _____

          Total words: _____

                        ಹ ೖ

Project   **Date & Time**

Word Count End: _____

- Word Count Begin: _____

          Total words: _____

                        ಹ ೖ

Project   **Date & Time**

Word Count End: _____

- Word Count Begin: _____

          Total words: _____

                        ಹ ೖ

Project   **Date & Time**

Word Count End: _____

- Word Count Begin: _____

        Total words: _____

                  ॐ ॐ

Project   **Date & Time**

Word Count End: _____

- Word Count Begin: _____

        Total words: _____

                  ॐ ॐ

Project   **Date & Time**

Word Count End: _____

- Word Count Begin: _____

        Total words: _____

                  ॐ ॐ

Project   **Date & Time**

Word Count End: _____

- Word Count Begin: _____

        Total words: _____

                  ॐ ॐ

Project   **Date & Time**

Word Count End: _____

- Word Count Begin: _____

        Total words: _____

ॐ ॐ

Project   **Date & Time**

Word Count End: _____

- Word Count Begin: _____

        Total words: _____

ॐ ॐ

Project   **Date & Time**

Word Count End: _____

- Word Count Begin: _____

        Total words: _____

ॐ ॐ

Project   **Date & Time**

Word Count End: _____

- Word Count Begin: _____

        Total words: _____

ॐ ॐ

Project　　　　　　　　**Date & Time**

Word Count End:　　　　　　_____

- Word Count Begin:　　　　_____

　　　　Total words:　　　　_____

ॐ ॐ

Project　　　　　　　　**Date & Time**

Word Count End:　　　　　　_____

- Word Count Begin:　　　　_____

　　　　Total words:　　　　_____

ॐ ॐ

Project　　　　　　　　**Date & Time**

Word Count End:　　　　　　_____

- Word Count Begin:　　　　_____

　　　　Total words:　　　　_____

ॐ ॐ

Project　　　　　　　　**Date & Time**

Word Count End:　　　　　　_____

- Word Count Begin:　　　　_____

　　　　Total words:　　　　_____

ॐ ॐ

Project   **Date & Time**

Word Count End: _____

- Word Count Begin: _____

       Total words: _____

ಹ ೕ

Project   **Date & Time**

Word Count End: _____

- Word Count Begin: _____

       Total words: _____

ಹ ೕ

Project   **Date & Time**

Word Count End: _____

- Word Count Begin: _____

       Total words: _____

ಹ ೕ

Project   **Date & Time**

Word Count End: _____

- Word Count Begin: _____

       Total words: _____

ಹ ೕ

Project   **Date & Time**

Word Count End: _____

- Word Count Begin: _____

       Total words: _____

                🙠 🙢

Project   **Date & Time**

Word Count End: _____

- Word Count Begin: _____

       Total words: _____

                🙠 🙢

Project   **Date & Time**

Word Count End: _____

- Word Count Begin: _____

       Total words: _____

                🙠 🙢

Project   **Date & Time**

Word Count End: _____

- Word Count Begin: _____

       Total words: _____

                🙠 🙢

Project   **Date & Time**

Word Count End: _____

- Word Count Begin: _____

        Total words: _____

ক্ষ ক্ষ

Project   **Date & Time**

Word Count End: _____

- Word Count Begin: _____

        Total words: _____

ক্ষ ক্ষ

Project   **Date & Time**

Word Count End: _____

- Word Count Begin: _____

        Total words: _____

ক্ষ ক্ষ

Project   **Date & Time**

Word Count End: _____

- Word Count Begin: _____

        Total words: _____

ক্ষ ক্ষ

Project   **Date & Time**

Word Count End: _____

\- Word Count Begin: _____

         Total words: _____

ॐ ॐ

Project   **Date & Time**

Word Count End: _____

\- Word Count Begin: _____

         Total words: _____

ॐ ॐ

Project   **Date & Time**

Word Count End: _____

\- Word Count Begin: _____

         Total words: _____

ॐ ॐ

Project   **Date & Time**

Word Count End: _____

\- Word Count Begin: _____

         Total words: _____

ॐ ॐ

Project   **Date & Time**

Word Count End: _____

- Word Count Begin: _____

      Total words: _____

ৰ্চ ৵

Project   **Date & Time**

Word Count End: _____

- Word Count Begin: _____

      Total words: _____

ৰ্চ ৵

Project   **Date & Time**

Word Count End: _____

- Word Count Begin: _____

      Total words: _____

ৰ্চ ৵

Project   **Date & Time**

Word Count End: _____

- Word Count Begin: _____

      Total words: _____

ৰ্চ ৵

Project   **Date & Time**

Word Count End: _____

- Word Count Begin: _____

          Total words: _____

                     ✷ ✷

Project   **Date & Time**

Word Count End: _____

- Word Count Begin: _____

          Total words: _____

                     ✷ ✷

Project   **Date & Time**

Word Count End: _____

- Word Count Begin: _____

          Total words: _____

                     ✷ ✷

Project   **Date & Time**

Word Count End: _____

- Word Count Begin: _____

          Total words: _____

                     ✷ ✷

Project   **Date & Time**

Word Count End: _____

- Word Count Begin: _____

        Total words: _____

                    ತ್ಠ ೞ

Project   **Date & Time**

Word Count End: _____

- Word Count Begin: _____

        Total words: _____

                    ತ್ಠ ೞ

Project   **Date & Time**

Word Count End: _____

- Word Count Begin: _____

        Total words: _____

                    ತ್ಠ ೞ

Project   **Date & Time**

Word Count End: _____

- Word Count Begin: _____

        Total words: _____

                    ತ್ಠ ೞ

Project   **Date & Time**

Word Count End: _____

- Word Count Begin: _____

          Total words: _____

ॐ ॐ

Project   **Date & Time**

Word Count End: _____

- Word Count Begin: _____

          Total words: _____

ॐ ॐ

Project   **Date & Time**

Word Count End: _____

- Word Count Begin: _____

          Total words: _____

ॐ ॐ

Project   **Date & Time**

Word Count End: _____

- Word Count Begin: _____

          Total words: _____

ॐ ॐ

Project   **Date & Time**

Word Count End: _____

\- Word Count Begin: _____

          Total words: _____

ॐ ॐ

Project   **Date & Time**

Word Count End: _____

\- Word Count Begin: _____

          Total words: _____

ॐ ॐ

Project   **Date & Time**

Word Count End: _____

\- Word Count Begin: _____

          Total words: _____

ॐ ॐ

Project   **Date & Time**

Word Count End: _____

\- Word Count Begin: _____

          Total words: _____

ॐ ॐ

Project   **Date & Time**

Word Count End: _____

- Word Count Begin: _____

       Total words: _____

                                              ಡಿ ೲ

Project   **Date & Time**

Word Count End: _____

- Word Count Begin: _____

       Total words: _____

                                              ಡಿ ೲ

Project   **Date & Time**

Word Count End: _____

- Word Count Begin: _____

       Total words: _____

                                              ಡಿ ೲ

Project   **Date & Time**

Word Count End: _____

- Word Count Begin: _____

       Total words: _____

                                              ಡಿ ೲ

Project   **Date & Time**

Word Count End: _____

\- Word Count Begin: _____

         Total words: _____

                         ॐ ॐ

Project   **Date & Time**

Word Count End: _____

\- Word Count Begin: _____

         Total words: _____

                         ॐ ॐ

Project   **Date & Time**

Word Count End: _____

\- Word Count Begin: _____

         Total words: _____

                         ॐ ॐ

Project   **Date & Time**

Word Count End: _____

\- Word Count Begin: _____

         Total words: _____

                         ॐ ॐ

Project   **Date & Time**

Word Count End: _____

- Word Count Begin: _____

         Total words: _____

             ❧ ❧

Project   **Date & Time**

Word Count End: _____

- Word Count Begin: _____

         Total words: _____

             ❧ ❧

Project   **Date & Time**

Word Count End: _____

- Word Count Begin: _____

         Total words: _____

             ❧ ❧

Project   **Date & Time**

Word Count End: _____

- Word Count Begin: _____

         Total words: _____

             ❧ ❧

Project   **Date & Time**

Word Count End: _____

- Word Count Begin: _____

       Total words: _____

                                    ☙ ❧

Project   **Date & Time**

Word Count End: _____

- Word Count Begin: _____

       Total words: _____

                                    ☙ ❧

Project   **Date & Time**

Word Count End: _____

- Word Count Begin: _____

       Total words: _____

                                    ☙ ❧

Project   **Date & Time**

Word Count End: _____

- Word Count Begin: _____

       Total words: _____

                                    ☙ ❧

Project   **Date & Time**

Word Count End: _____

\- Word Count Begin: _____

         Total words: _____

꙰ ꙰

Project   **Date & Time**

Word Count End: _____

\- Word Count Begin: _____

         Total words: _____

꙰ ꙰

Project   **Date & Time**

Word Count End: _____

\- Word Count Begin: _____

         Total words: _____

꙰ ꙰

Project   **Date & Time**

Word Count End: _____

\- Word Count Begin: _____

         Total words: _____

꙰ ꙰